Ramadan Acti

Written by Comilita M. Salah

Edited by Kathleen Kehl Lewis

Illustrated by Ben DeSoto

Cover Art by Cheri Macoubrie Wilson

Table of Contents

Introduction

The old saying "good things come in small packages" is an apt description of this holiday booklet. This book is packed with all types of projects and ideas for making Ramadan a special time or for simply learning about a cultural event of importance. Teaching opportunities abound in these pages including an overview of Islam and Ramadan, creative activities and crafts, learning games, and extension activities and resources to allow children to further explore the Islamic holy month of Ramadan.

Teacher Created Resources, Inc.

6421 Industry Way

Westminster, CA 92683

www.teachercreated.com

©*2000 Teacher Created Resources, Inc.*

Reprinted, 2006

Made in U.S.A.

ISBN 13: 978-1-57690-609-5

Islam: A Brief Overview

Islam is the religion of the Muslims. It began in 610 A.D. when Allah (the Arabic word for God) revealed the Qur'an (the Muslim Holy Book) to Prophet Muhammed, peace be upon him. (Muslims always say "peace be upon him" when mentioning the name of a prophet.) The word *Islam* means peace and submission to the One God—Allah. Muslims are those who submit to Allah.

There are more than 1.25 billion Muslims on Earth, and Islam is the fastest growing religion in the world. Although many believe that all or most of the Muslims are Arab, the majority of the Muslim population calls Southeast Asia home. Indonesia, Malaysia, and Pakistan are the largest Muslim countries. The Middle East accounts for only about twenty-five percent of the world's Muslims.

Islam is based on five pillars: Tawhid—Faith in One God; Salat—the five daily prayers; Zakat—obligatory payment to the poor; Sawm—fasting the month of Ramadan; and Hajj—making a pilgrimage to the Ka'ba in Mecca. By saying "I bear witness that there is no god but Allah and that Muhammed is His servant and messenger," one declares his or her faith and becomes a Muslim. Thereafter, the Muslim performs all of the required duties to the best of his or her ability in the hopes of increasing faith, getting closer to Allah, and eventually going to Heaven.

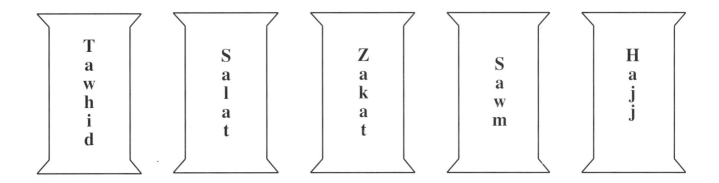

Beside the five basic Islamic duties, Muslims must perform other good deeds in the community. For example, one is required to give in charity to those less fortunate, to be kind and generous to one's family, and to take care of one's parents in their old age.

Muslims have many beliefs in common with other religious groups. They believe in the Prophets: Adam, Abraham, Noah, Moses, and Jesus (peace be upon them), among others. Honesty is valued highly in Islam. Having a close-knit family unit is also very important. Islam forbids killing, stealing, the use of alcohol and drugs, and any other act that harms society. Muslims believe in working hard, doing the best possible job, and wanting for one's neighbors what one wants for oneself.

Many Muslim men and women are doctors, lawyers, engineers, and teachers. They want to be good, productive members of American society and to be good examples for our nation's children. Truly, Muslims have added another important thread to this fabric we call America.

Ramadan–The Month of Fasting

For Muslims, no time of the year is more anticipated than the holy month of fasting—Ramadan. Ramadan is the ninth month of the Islamic year. During this month, Muslims all over the world abstain from food, drink, and marital relations from dawn until sunset.

While children are not required to fast until the age of puberty, many as young as six or seven wish to join the fast. Allah requires every adult to observe the fast except for those who are traveling, sick, or elderly. They are permitted to break the fast and make up the days by fasting later.

Fasting, for Muslims, is a way of getting closer to Allah by practicing patience, self-control, and restraint. While denying the body food and drink, the Muslim is free to focus his or her time and energy on reading the Qur'an, performing extra prayer, and increasing his or her good deeds. Muslims must also take extra care not to lose their temper or use foul language, as these would nullify the fast and require repetition of that day. It is truly a time of spiritual growth, introspection, and inner joy and peace.

Curan

The Mosque (or Masjid—the Muslim place of worship) is a very crowded place during the month of Ramadan. Many Muslims rush to the Mosque at sunset to break their fast together. After the evening prayer, they enjoy a humble meal and resume their prayers. Every night during this special month, congregational prayers are held in which a large section of the Qur'an is read.

After a long night of prayer, the Muslim awakens early, before dawn, to have a small morning meal before the dawn prayer. Then a new day of fasting and rewards begins.

With the sighting of the new moon, the fast is over and the Eid-ul-Fitr, or Holiday of the Feast, begins. Muslims begin the three-day celebration with a mid-morning congregational prayer. Then they spend the rest of the holiday visiting friends and family, giving gifts, and, of course, eating!

Comprehension Questions

Circle the correct answer.

1. True   False   Prophet Muhammed (peace be upon him) wrote the Qur'an.

2. True   False   Most of the world's Muslims live in the Middle East.

3. True   False   Islam is based on five pillars: faith, prayer, poor-due, fasting, and pilgrimage.

4. True   False   Muslims do not believe in Adam and Moses (peace be upon them).

5. True   False   Muslims contribute to society as doctors, lawyers, and teachers.

Write a short answer.

6. Why do Muslims look forward to the month of Ramadan? _____

_____

7. What are some additional duties performed by Muslims during Ramadan? _____

_____

8. Describe a typical day for someone who is fasting. _____

_____

_____

9. How do Muslims know when the month of fasting ends? _____

_____

10. From what age is a person required to fast? _____

11. How do Muslims celebrate the Eid-ul-Fitr? Are any of your holiday celebrations similar?

_____

_____

12. Ramadan holds special significance for Muslims. What times of the year are especially important to you? _____

_____

13. Compare and contrast Islam with your religion. How are they alike and different?

_____

_____

14. In which countries are the majority of the people Muslim? _____

_____

15. How many countries in the world seem to have no Muslims? _____

Ramadan Word Search

```
S  O  M  H  U  M  B  L  E  E  T  H  I  I  N  K  T  H
E  A  T  T  C  O  N  T  R  O  L  H  M  N  I  P  I  S
U  I  S  A  R  A  S  E  L  O  R  U  A  Z  A  R  N  N
Q  U  R  A  N  A  G  E  P  A  S  L  E  R  R  A  C  S
S  T  I  N  F  E  I  S  T  L  H  E  E  E  C  N  R  A
O  P  I  N  E  R  D  L  I  H  C  N  Y  A  T  Y  E  C
M  A  G  H  R  E  B  M  A  L  T  A  O  S  O  L  A  R
F  T  H  C  E  A  S  M  I  S  R  D  R  Q  D  P  S  O
L  E  A  S  O  T  M  B  U  P  T  A  T  H  A  E  E  W
M  L  U  N  A  R  T  A  H  R  L  E  A  T  R  N  E  D
N  D  O  O  T  I  Z  B  D  L  E  T  I  S  O  T  B  E
I  A  N  T  M  H  E  O  I  A  U  E  R  O  L  R  D  D
S  T  A  A  I  I  L  P  H  T  N  O  M  T  E  O  T  F
H  E  L  E  L  F  A  R  E  C  A  S  T  A  A  N  L  D
D  S  O  N  K  T  P  L  E  A  Y  G  K  U  E  E  W  I
I  O  E  O  N  G  R  G  N  I  T  H  G  I  S  S  T  E
```

Below are 25 words associated with Ramadan. Find them in this word search and improve your cultural awareness.

Ramadan	pillars	increase	humble	crowded
sighting	milk	Qur'an	patience	children
Maghreb	month	lunar	break	self
parents	moon	Muslims	solar	dates
control	prayer	Mosques	fast	Islam

Ramadan Activity Calendar

Sunday	Monday	Tuesday	Wednesday	Thursday	Friday	Saturday
1 Journal: How can you help the poor in your area?	**2** List five reasons why you love your parents.	**3** Complete this: "If everyone had more self-control…"	**4** Name four things for which you are grateful.	**5** Journal: "One way I hope to improve the world is…"	**6** Interview a Muslim in your area about the difficulties faced due to a different culture.	**7** Compare Islam to another religion. What are the similarities and differences?
8 Find a way to help the needy in your area and do it.	**9** Journal: Pretend you are fasting. Write about your experience.	**10** Tell each person in your house three things you like about them.	**11** Make an extra effort to be kind to those around you.	**12** Plan to spend an afternoon volunteering with the elderly.	**13** Help your family with chores that you normally do not do.	**14** Volunteer to shovel your neighbor's snow or to do yard work.
15 Write a letter to your grandparents or special relatives.	**16** Volunteer to serve food to the poor.	**17** Journal: "The most important part of my life is…"	**18** Create a Ramadan display for your classroom.	**19** Make a list of ways to better spend your time.	**20** Volunteer to tutor other students at your school.	**21** Visit the museum. Locate displays about Muslims.
22 Donate a portion of your allowance to a charitable cause.	**23** Spend your evening without television. Read a book instead.	**24** Journal: What does **charity** mean to you?	**25** Visit a Muslim professional. Discuss how fasting affects his or life.	**26** Write a Thank You note to your parents for all they have done for you.	**27** Create a Myth vs. Reality poster on Islam and Muslims.	**28** Make your parents breakfast in bed.
29 Go to a Middle Eastern restaurant for dinner.	**30** Journal: Write about your Ramadan experience.	Share the Ramadan experience with your Muslim neighbors by participating in these daily activities.				

* The beginning of the Islamic Calendar month is confirmed by actual sighting of the moon. See page 15 (Extension Activities) for finding the exact start date of Ramadan.

Make Your Own Tasbih

It was a tradition of Prophet Muhammed (peace be upon him) to make special supplications at the end of each of the five daily prayers. Some such supplications are: "God is Great," "Glory to God," and "Praise be to God." Muslims repeat each of these 33 times just as the Prophet did.

It has become common for a Muslim to use a string of 33 beads to count the times he or she makes each supplication.

Materials

- 33 beads of two or three colors (3/8" [.9 cm] or larger)
- yarn for stringing beads
- extra yarn for tassel
- scissors

Directions

After choosing your colored beads, create a color pattern for your beads. Thread the beads on the yarn until you have strung 33 beads. Keeping about two inches of yarn as a reserve, tie a knot in the yarn and cut. To make the tassel, cut several pieces of yarn about six inches (15 cm) in length. Fold the pieces in half over the knot. Use another piece of yarn to wrap around the knot and string. Tie in a knot. Now you are ready to use your Tasbih!

Though commonly called "prayer beads," Tasbih are also sometimes called "worry beads." You can use your Tasbih to help you think about something that worries you or just to count the things you have to be grateful for in your life.

"An Ordinary Day" Instructions

The purpose of this game is to provide students an exciting way to gain insight into the day-to-day life of a Muslim child. While some daily activities are different, most are the same as those done by any typical child.

Teacher Instructions

Copy the gameboard and laminate it. You may also wish to color the spaces on the board.

Materials:

- 2 to 4 markers (buttons, paper scraps, etc.)
- 1 die
- gameboard

Rules of the Game

The object is to be the first to finish the night prayer by reaching the end of the gameboard.

1. Each player rolls the die, and the player who rolls the highest number plays first. Play rotates to the right.

2. Players take turns rolling the die and moving the indicated number of spaces.

3. The player reads and follows the instructions of the space on which he or she lands.

4. Play continues until someone finishes the night prayer, by reaching the end of the gameboard.

5. To win, the player must land exactly on the "You Win!" space. For example, if a player is two spaces away and rolls a 3, the player loses that turn and must try to roll the exact number on the next turn.

"An OrdinaryDay" Gameboard

Start	You wake up on time for the dawn (Fajr) prayer. Move Ahead 2 Spaces.	You help your family by making the beds before school. Roll Again.		You do not properly wash (wudu) for prayer. Lose a Turn.		You do not complete your Math homework. Move Back 3 Spaces.		Refreshed by your ablution, you perform the noon (Duhr) prayer with your classmates. Roll Again.	You are late for the noon (Duhr) prayer. Lose a Turn.
									☆BONUS☆ Switch places with the player in 1st place. If that's you, move ahead one space.
You miss your bus and are late to the afternoon (Asr) prayer. Go Back 4 Spaces.	You complete your homework before dinner and can go outside to play. Move Ahead 2 Spaces.	You refuse to help with the dinner dishes. Lose a Turn.			Because you read the Qur'an during your recess, you earn good deeds. Jump Ahead 3 Spaces.		After completing your schoolwork, you help tutor other students. Move Ahead 1 Space .		
Your homework needs more attention. Go Back 4 Spaces.	It's time for the evening (Maghreb) prayer and you are on time! Move Ahead 1 Space.		Instead of practicing your Islamic History, you watch TV for 2 hours. Lose a Turn.	You help your little brother with his homework. Roll Again.		You do not study for the science test and get a bad grade. Go Back 3 Spaces.		You have finished your night ('Isha) prayer! You Win!

"An Ordinary

Start	You wake up on time for the dawn (Fajr) prayer. Move Ahead 2 Spaces.	You help your family by making the beds before school. Roll Again.		You do not properly wash (wudu) for prayer. Lose a Turn.

You miss your bus and are late to the afternoon (Asr) prayer. Go Back 4 Spaces.	You complete your homework before dinner and can go outside to play. Move Ahead 2 Spaces.		You refuse to help with the dinner dishes. Lose a Turn.	

Your homework needs more attention. Go Back 4 Spaces.		It's time for the evening (Maghreb) prayer and you are on time! Move Ahead 1 Space.		Instead of practicing your Islamic History, you watch TV for 2 hours. Lose a Turn.

Day" Gameboard

	You do not complete your Math homework. Move Back 3 Spaces.		Refreshed by your ablution, you perform the noon (Duhr) prayer with your classmates. Roll Again.	You are late for the noon (Duhr) prayer. Lose a Turn.
				☆BONUS☆ Switch places with the player in 1ˢᵀ place. If that's you, move ahead one space.
	Because you read the Qur'an during your recess, you earn good deeds. Jump Ahead 3 Spaces.		After completing your schoolwork, you help tutor other students. Move Ahead 1 Space.	

You help your little brother with his homework. Roll Again.		You do not study for the science test and get a bad grade. Go Back 3 Spaces.		You have finished your night ('Isha) prayer! You Win!

Write Your Name in Arabic

The study of the Arabic language is important for Muslims because the Qur'an is written in Arabic. Unlike English, Arabic is written from right to left. Use this chart of letters to write your name in Arabic.

At the end of a word	In the middle of a word	At beginning of a word	Letter Alone	English Equivalent
ا	ا	أ	أ	a
ب	ب	ب	ب	b
ت	ت	ت	ت	t
ث	ث	ث	ث	th (think)
ج	ج	ج	ج	j
ح	ح	ح	ح	H
خ	خ	خ	خ	kh
د	د	د	د	d
ذ	ذ	ذ	ذ	th (this)
ر	ر	ر	ر	r
ز	ز	ز	ز	z
س	س	س	س	s
ش	ش	ش	ش	sh
ص	ص	ص	ص	S
ض	ض	ض	ض	TH
ط	ط	ط	ط	ta
ظ	ظ	ظ	ظ	Dh
ع	ع	ع	ع	"none"
غ	غ	غ	غ	gh
ف	ف	ف	ف	f
ق	ق	ق	ق	q
ك	ك	ك	ك	k
ل	ل	ل	ل	l
م	م	م	م	m
ن	ن	ن	ن	n
ه	ه	ه	ه	h
و	و	و	و	w
ي	ي	ي	ي	y

If your name is Dan, for example, it would be written like this: دان

Now let's practice!

How would you write the name Arnold? "أرنالد" is correct!

Don't forget, when writing your name think of how the letters sound and write from right to left.

Now try writing your name and the names of your friends and family members in Arabic.

_____

_____

_____

_____

_____

_____

_____

_____

_____

_____

_____

_____

An "A-Mazing" Trip to the Mosque

Help Iman find her way to the Mosque before Eid-ul-Fitr prayer starts.

Muslim World Matching

Below are the names of some countries where at least half of the people are Muslims. On the next page are outline maps of those countries, in random order. Color the maps, using colored pencils or crayons. Then cut out each square along the dotted lines. Use an atlas or a world map to help you to match each country to its name.

Pakistan	**Malaysia**	**Indonesia**
Saudi Arabia	**Iran**	**Afghanistan**
Libya	**Tunisia**	**Somalia**
Sudan	**Egypt**	**Jordan**
Turkey	**Nigeria**	**Albania**

 #2609 Ramadan Activities

Muslim World Matching *(cont.)*

Once you have determined which country name matches which map outline, you can use the cards to play a "memory" game. Mix up all the cards (maps and names) and place them facedown. Each player takes a turn turning over two cards to see if they match. Play continues until all the cards have been matched. When you have mastered these countries, you can make the game more challenging by creating another set of cards showing the flags of the different countries.

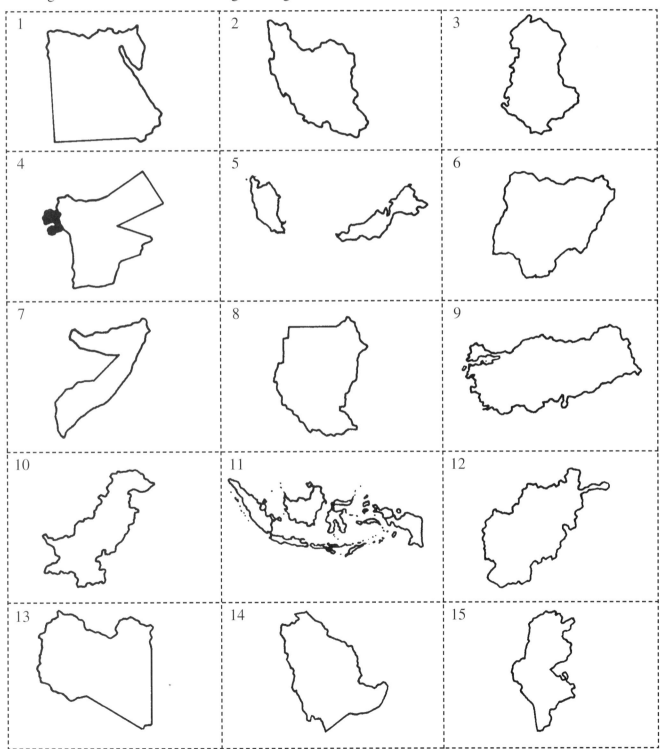

Extension Activities

1. Have students find out more about Ramadan. They can use one of the resource books below to write a report on this holy month.

2. Have students write a report on a country with a majority Muslim population. Tell them to try to choose a country that was not used in the matching game. They will compare and contrast that society with the United States.

3. Every major city in the United States has at least one mosque. Plan a field trip to a mosque in your area. Call and arrange to see a congregational prayer.

4. Have students use the Arabic alphabet to send and decode secret messages.

5. Have students find how many words they can make from the letters in "Eid Mubarak." This greeting is used by Muslims around the world on the day of Eid-ul-Fitr and for many days later.

6. Search the newspaper for stories concerning Ramadan and Eid-ul-Fitr. Share with the class.

7. Invite members of the Muslim community to come and speak to the class.

8. Contact the Islamic Society of North America (ISNA) at P.O. Box 38, Plainfield, IN 46168-0038, or at *www.isna.net* to find out the exact starting date of Ramadan. You can also contact this number to find a mosque in your area.

Resources

Ali, Aminah Ibrahim. *The Three Muslim Festivals*. IQRA International Education Foundation, 1998.

Choudhury, G.W. *Islam and the Contemporary World*. Kazi Publications, 1994.

Haneef, Suzanne. *What Everyone Should Know About Islam and the Muslims*. Kazi Publications, 1995.

Holy Qur'an. Kazi Publications, 1998.

Answer Keys

Comprehension Questions

1. False

2. False

3. True

4. False

5. True

6. Answers will vary.

7. Answers will vary but should include extra prayers and reading the Qur'an.

8. Answers will vary.

9. By the sighting of the new moon in the ninth month of the Islamic year.

10. from the age of puberty

11. They celebrate with prayer and then a feast. Answers will vary.

12. Answers will vary.

13. Answers will vary.

14. Answers will vary.

15. None. Although they may be a minority, Muslims can be found in every country.

Ramadan Word Search

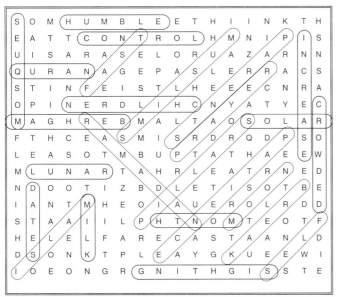

An "A-Mazing" Trip to the Mosque

Muslim World Matching

1. Egypt
2. Iran
3. Albania
4. Jordan
5. Malaysia
6. Nigeria
7. Somalia
8. Sudan
9. Turkey
10. Pakistan
11. Indonesia
12. Afghanistan
13. Libya
14. Saudi Arabia
15. Tunisia